More Praise

"The church desperately needs robust theological reflection on human sexuality. *Holy Love* is a thoughtful overture for the rest of us."

—James C. Howell, senior pastor, Myers Park United Methodist Church, Charlotte, NC; author, *Weak Enough to Lead*

"This book is not merely another rope in a fierce tug-of-war over biblical authority and human sexuality. With his trademark style, Steve Harper offers a wise, compassionate, and deeply Wesleyan perspective on biblical interpretation and LGBTQIA+ inclusion. Read this book, study it with others, and keep it on your shelf for regular reference."

—Magrey R. deVega, senior pastor, Hyde Park United Methodist Church, Tampa, FL

"I am often asked for a book study that gets to grips with what scripture says—and doesn't say—about same-gender relationships, and I will be so grateful to be able to point people to this one!"

—Helen Ryde, southeastern regional organizer, Reconciling Ministry Network, Chicago, IL

"'Love must be the North Star in our theological sky and the anchor in our spirit as we advocate on behalf of LGBTQ people.' Who could disagree with Steve Harper even if they oppose the ecclesial and personal reform his life and his line of biblical interpretation commend? Which I do not. As a concise biblical theology, readers will likely find the claims of *Holy Love* at times sturdy and in places worthy of deeper investigation. Yet the canopy of insights he presents are rooted in clear Christian conviction and help clarify a constellation of questions about human sexuality and the Bible."

—Gerald C. Liu, Assistant Professor of Worship and Preaching, Princeton Theological Seminary, Princeton, NJ; Elder, Mississippi Annual Conference, UMC

"In all our church fighting about what is and is not incompatible with Christian teaching, Christians seem to have forgotten the core of Christian teaching—that is, we're all incompatible with Christian teaching. Not one of us is found compatible. Rather, we are made compatible by God's grace. In *Holy Love*, Steve Harper reminds Christians that married love is holy precisely because it's an arena where life with another exposes the stranger you call *you* to the unmerited forgiveness of the other who knows your worst self. Marriage, as the wedding rite makes clear, is about sanctification; therefore, to deny committed couples, gay or straight, marriage deprives them not of a privilege but of a medicine. *Holy Love* provides pastors and parishioners the biblical and theological resources to have a holy conversation about how that medicine may be administered to same-sex couples too and how their marriages might also serve as parables for how God loves us all."

—Jason Micheli, head pastor, Annandale United Methodist Church, Annandale, VA; blogger, tamedcynic.org

"Steve Harper invites us to step back from the 'clobber' passages and begin our theology of human sexuality with a comprehensive consideration of the nature of our Creator, Christ, the Spirit, the creation, the church, the Trinity, the covenant, grace, and humanity. As one who has made a too-slow journey from my own excluding, selective literalism to a theology of full inclusion, I wish I had read this book twenty-five years ago. An honest reading of Steve's thorough treatment of the biblical texts and theology of covenant love may woo you away from culturally driven preconceived notions."

—Paul Purdue, senior pastor, Belmont United Methodist Church, Nashville, TN

Steve Harper

HOLY LOVE

A BIBLICAL THEOLOGY FOR HUMAN SEXUALITY

Abingdon Press™
Nashville

HOLY LOVE:
A Biblical Theology for Human Sexuality

Copyright © 2019 by Steve Harper

All rights reserved.

Library of Congress Cataloging-in-Publication Data has been requested.

ISBN 978-1-5018-9608-8

Scripture quotations unless noted otherwise are from the Common English Bible. Copyright © 2011 by the Common English Bible. All rights reserved. Used by permission. www.Common EnglishBible.com

Scripture quotations marked (NRSV) are taken from the New Revised Standard Version of the Bible, copyright 1989, Division of Christian Education of the National Council of the Churches of Christ in the United States of America. Used by permission. All rights reserved.

19 20 21 22 23 24 25 26 27 28 29—10 9 8 7 6 5 4 3 2 1
MANUFACTURED IN THE UNITED STATES OF AMERICA

CONTENTS

AND SO IT BEGAN

One after another they told their stories. Twenty-three of them. All stories of rejection from other Christians once they identified themselves as LGBTQ people.[1] Some were rejected by their parents when they came out. Some were shunned by siblings and other family members. Some were marginalized by coworkers. And some who had held positions of lay and ordained ministry were told to clean out their desks and vacate the building. Most had experienced more than one type of rejection. But all of them were still Christians, still fully devoted followers of Jesus Christ. And all of them were holding on to the hope that one day the church might believe differently about them and relate in new ways to them.

I had been invited by members of two LGBTQ Christian groups in Orlando to meet with them shortly after I wrote *For the Sake of the Bride*.[2] They wanted to hear my story of how I came to think differently about LGBTQ people and to describe the theology that was now defining and directing my life and ministry. But I had not been in the room with these good and godly folks very long before I realized that I was not there to tell them my story. I was there to listen to theirs. And so it began.

ONE

THE JOURNEY

T heology arises from something prior to itself—a cultural concern, a pressing issue, a personal interest, a communal challenge. This is one reason why John Wesley made experience part of his theological interpretation, by adding to the already-existing Anglican trilateral of scripture, tradition, and reason. Experience was his way of noting that theology is not ultimately about belief but rather about life. Theology does not exist in a vacuum; it emerges from somewhere, and it takes us someplace. And if it is worth its salt, theology always takes us to a new place (even while confirming previous things), to a place where our lives expand more deeply and widely, and where we mature.

John Wesley called this kind of theology "living faith." He understood that in some respects theology is always autobiographical. Theologians are apostles (messengers), sent in their times and to their places to declare what they have seen and heard (Acts 4:20). Their theology inevitably emerges from their vantage point, and it expresses their deepest convictions. In this sense, theology can never be impersonal, even as it can never be independent. This is especially true in relation to a theology (establishing divine guidance) for how human beings experience sexuality.

To set this book in its proper context, I must first tell you about the journey I have been on—a journey that spans decades, a journey that took me from one place with respect to sexuality and located me in a new place. My theology of sexuality is taking me somewhere.[1] It is, and continues to be, a journey.[2]

In ways going back into my childhood, I see how God has been at work to bring me to the place where I am now. My parents taught and modeled love for all people. My educational experiences helped to shape an inclusive world view. My marriage to Jeannie (who was and is in her own right loving and inclusive of all, out of an upbringing in an Air Force family) has given me the perspective and motivation to be inclusive. In all these ways and more, the seeds were sown for the theology of sexuality you will read about in this book.

But as a church leader, I traveled another path—the path of theological conservativism. To this day, I remain orthodox (despite some allegations otherwise), and when that played out with respect to sexuality, it meant heteronormativity. I lived in that world from 1965 (when I was licensed to preach) in the Methodist Church until 2014. Sometimes I gave very little attention to a theology of sexuality. But when it became a focal point during the institutional formation of The United Methodist Church in 1972, I joined with so many others (in the denomination and in the culture, which was also focusing on homosexuality) in developing my beliefs about sexuality.

The change in the UMC occurred while I was a student at Asbury Theological Seminary. The institution revised its ethos statement more directly to reflect the language of homosexual practice as incompatible with Christian faith. Sexuality was a topic to be discussed on campus, not surprisingly within the context of that ethos statement and in the larger context of conservative Christianity. At that time, I had no reason to doubt the legitimacy of what my denomination was doing or disbelieve what my professors were teaching me. I accepted these secondary witnesses. Like a typical seminarian, I trusted my teachers and was too busy reading books, writing papers, and taking tests to do firsthand exploration on my own. I graduated in 1973 under the influence of a conservative theology of sexuality.[3] That theology was given additional shape by writings of the leaders of the Good News caucus, which had been formed in 1967 to offer a critique of what they felt to be liberal erosion in United Methodism.

I had not been in pastoral ministry long before leaders of Good News invited me to serve on the board. I forget what specifically prompted the invitation, but I must surely have been saying and doing things that made me attractive to them. They were intent on having younger board members, and they reached out to me with an invitation to become a leader, which I accepted. My years on the Good News board brought me in contact with what was an even more concentrated conservatism in general, but also (and especially after 1972) a more exclusionary theology of sexuality. I marched in step with all of this, so much so that when a group of people planned a gathering in Atlanta (which became the Confessing Movement), I was asked to bring the opening address. To this day, I don't know how that happened, but it was an invitation I was happy to accept. I soon found myself involved in two groups whose theology of sexuality was conservative, both with respect to the compatibility of LGBTQ sexual practice in general, and, not long after, the added belief that LGBTQ people could not be ordained. As had been the case in seminary, I trusted my mentors and shared their views without taking the time to do my own homework, even believing that liberal authors and views were, to some extent, part of the problem that was leading The United Methodist Church astray.[4]

My years at Duke University (1977–1980) took me out of the direct line of fire with respect to this matter. And in new space created by PhD work in historical theology and Wesley studies, I had the opportunity to view the Wesleyan tradition in a deeper and broader way. I was never told what to believe by my professors at Duke (which was itself different than the environment in which I had been living and ministering), but only that whatever I believed had to be confirmed by the Christian faith in general and the Wesleyan tradition in particular. My experience at Duke was a grace-filled gift in many ways.

I carried this educational and ministerial experience (1973–1980) with me back to Asbury Theological Seminary, where I had been invited to become a professor of spiritual formation and Wesley studies. I accepted that invitation over offers from several other schools. The lure of my alma mater was strong. I served from 1980 through the end of 2012 as a professor and administrator.

Ironically, my return to the seminary in 1980 included a request that I not be officially involved in the Good News caucus as I had been before. It was not a requirement for employment, but rather a desire on the part of the seminary's administration at that time. The Good News caucus had moved its headquarters to Wilmore, and the seminary did not want people to think that decision had been initiated or officially approved by the institution.[5] The seminary and Good News shared many theological perspectives, while maintaining separate institutional identities. I was happy to comply with the request because my aim in returning to Asbury was to be a theological professor, not a movement's proponent.

My return placed me back into the more exclusionary environment, put into print through the seminary's theological statement and especially in its ethos statement. I affirmed both. Meanwhile, as an encourager for spiritual formation, I became one of a few professors to whom our LGBTQ students turned in their struggles—specifically whether to remain enrolled in a school that was nonaffirming, and more generally how to integrate their call by God into some form of ordained ministry in denominations that refused to ordain LGBTQ people. Those students knew where I stood theologically, but they still viewed me (as I have come to learn from them) as a "safe professor" to converse about these things. Their subsequent support of my change of view has helped me to see that back in those days I was a person now referred to as "welcoming but not affirming." I am glad for the former, but still regretful for the latter. And beyond the label, I am grateful for those LGBTQ students who surfaced after Lent of 2014 to be among my best supporters.

For you to understand the rest of this book, it is important to see how deeply and how long I was embedded in a conservative theology of sexuality. In fact, that journey makes me an enigma to conservatives. They don't know what to do with me, even though I remain orthodox to this day. I know from communication with some leaders that I have become a threat to their position, because I have chosen to abandon much of what they teach about sexuality. And in a culture and church where LGBTQ matters are intensifying, I understand how they would view my transformation negatively. But I have also come to learn that their resistance is troubling, because some in their ranks have confided in me that they are also where I now am—though they are unable to speak and act accordingly. I have learned from these folks how institutionally intimidating the advocates of an exclusionary sexuality can be. So it is important for you to know that the thread of lament runs through this book for those who would like to be as outspoken as I have become but are convinced they cannot.

The journey I described thus far began to change years ago, but not with respect to sexuality. It began to change as the seeds sown in my PhD work in Wesleyan theology began to sprout and grow, and as a new wave of renewal began to sweep across the church—a movement now referred to as "emergence" Christianity.[6] As one devoted to the renewal of the church from the day of my conversion to Christ in 1963, I was drawn into this renewal movement like a moth to a flame. The initial leaders of that movement (e.g., Phyllis Tickle and Brian McLaren) became valued guides on my journey, and subsequent advocates (e.g., Jonathan Wilson-Hartgrove and Cheryl Anderson) have added depth and breadth to my overall theological perspectives. They have also strengthened my ties with longstanding mentors who have given me substantial guidance over the years (Thomas

Merton, E. Stanley Jones, Dorothy Day, Martin Luther King Jr., Oscar Romero, Richard Rohr, Barbara Brown Taylor, and so on), along with LGBTQ spokespersons whom I will refer to later in the book. Something was burning. My heart was being strangely warmed... again. And in Lent of 2014, it burst into flame with respect to a theology of sexuality. The first year in retirement had afforded me the time and space to ponder things more deeply.[7] Little did I know what that was about to mean.

Simply put, I entered Lent of 2014 as a "welcoming but not affirming" Christian and emerged from it on Easter Monday as an "all means all" Christian. It was a new place to stand, but I was not standing still; I was beginning the exploration of a new theological world, a journey that is ongoing.[8] The first step was an "enough is enough" experience, which I write about in *For the Sake of the Bride*.[9] That experience was a reaction to things being said and done in the larger church and within The United Methodist Church to disparage and demean LGBTQ people—things that I did not agree with, even in the context of my conservatism. I knew I had come to a fork in the road. I had not chosen a new path so much as a new path had been chosen for me. A new invitation was being extended, and I knew that I had to accept it. I did not know where the new road would take me; I only knew that I could not travel any further on the one I had been on for so long.

Sadly, some have caricatured my Lenten experience as a vague, ethereal, mystical experience. But as I write clearly in *For the Sake of the Bride*, it was anything but that![10] Far from being a "shaft of light" that illuminated my darkened soul, the experience was a direct encounter with prayers in *The Book of Common Prayer*, prayers that in their text exhorted those praying them to come to grips with the harm being done in the body of Christ by our many divisions and the great dangers we were putting the church in through our contentious partisanship. I came to the place where I knew I either had to honor the prayers—or stop praying them. Rather than being an intangible impression, it was the most textually based experience I've ever had. Instead of being something formless, it was an experience that emerged from a collision between my praying the written prayers and having to come to grips with what I was praying about.

The initial experience soon evolved into a sense of call to be a visible ally with and advocate for LGBTQ people, again not in a mystical way but in a rational and intentional way—a way that commenced with the writing of *For the Sake of the Bride*. This enactment was not different from the way I had sought to live the Christian life the previous fifty-one years; it was consistent with it. Friends know that I have informally and half-humorously said that "The Hokey Pokey" should be included in the next edition of *The United Methodist Hymnal*. And without belaboring that point, you know it ends with the verse that says we must "put our whole self in . . . and shake it all about . . . that's what it's all about." My experience during Lent of 2014 was an encounter with the living God that admitted nothing less than a hokey-pokey response.

But I must tell you, it felt strange—and still does in some ways. For one thing, I felt like Paul when he said he was the chief of sinners (1 Tim 1:15). For decades, I had owned and advanced a conservative theology of sexuality. I could nether count nor remember how many times I had spoken or written from that vantage point, and I still have no idea how many LGBTQ people I have harmed over those years. No matter what you think about the chapters of this book, you must not think I am writing from any recently assumed high ground. By no means! This book is the writing of a "mea culpa" confession as much as it is a constructive theological explanation from scripture. Hopefully, what I have written in the preceding pages confirms that.

I felt like those in Jesus's parable who began laboring in the vineyard late in the day (Matt 20:1-16). So many labored longer and harder as LGBTQ people and allies in the work of attempting to make the church more inclusive. I am a bona fide latecomer. This realization would have stopped me in my tracks, except for one thing: there were latecomers working in the vineyard in Jesus's parable. And more, they were invited to go to work late in the day without reference to those who had worked more than they had. And if that were not enough, the parable revealed that when payment time came, everyone was paid the same wage. The point of the whole parable is this: it is not how long anyone works in the vineyard, but what ultimately counts is that they work. There was no point in wondering why I didn't start working sooner; the only point was to go to work. I found myself singing along with Charles Wesley, "tis mercy all, immense and free, for O my God it found out me" and also "my chains fell off, my heart was free, I rose, went forth, and followed thee."[11] The following chapters are a description of the theology that emerges from a study of scripture, and the life that such a theology calls us to live in the world and in the church. I hope it will be an encouragement to those of you who are already on the journey—or an invitation to you to join it, no matter how late in the day.

Discussion

1. How would you describe your journey in which you came to the view of human sexuality that you currently hold? Where did you receive or obtain your views?

2. Have there been unexpected experiences in that journey?

3. As you encounter this book, what next steps do you want to take in your journey?

TWO

THE HERMENEUTIC

O ne of the biggest benefits from seminary education was learning inductive Bible study (IBS) methodology.[1] When I moved into pastoral ministry, I taught the method to participants in the churches and communities where I served. And for the first three years of teaching at Asbury Theological Seminary, I taught the introductory course in IBS, using the Gospel of John as the biblical text. I have used inductive study methodology almost every day since 1970.[2] When I changed my mind about sexuality in Lent of 2014, two key insights from inductive methodology became immediately significant and remain so to this day.

The first learning was the reminder that the differences between Christians about scripture are not disagreements about its authority but rather about its interpretation. The differences are not about revelation but about hermeneutics. Over and over, Robert Traina emphasized this, reminding us of the important truth that when we find ourselves in disagreement over something in the Bible, we are disagreeing as fellow Christians. He eschewed any attempt to use scripture in an attempt to gain high ground over any other Christian.

Sadly, much of the Christian world ignores this principle, choosing instead to allege that their group has the "biblical" view, and that other groups are "unbiblical" in varying degrees. This allegation is "a straw person," which is a falsehood based on knocking over a different interpretation by misconstruing it. But the allegation is a wedge driven between those who might have otherwise learned from those with whom they disagree if they had stayed together. In the ensuing years since I wrote *For the Sake of the Bride*,[3] the tendency to win votes in the debate as a contest between those who "believe the Bible" and those who "do not believe the Bible" lies at the heart of our inability (and lack of will) to find common ground on a theology of sexuality. Simply put, the pivot is not the inspiration and authority of scripture but its interpretation and application.

The second contribution is the first principle of the inductive method: study the text as a whole before exploring the parts. With reference to the Bible, Robert Traina described it this way: "The reader is urged to study the entire manual . . . before making a serious attempt to understand fully any of its parts."[4] This is also what we mean when we say, "A text without a context is a pretext." The first step in studying the Bible is to get the big picture. And since the topic or theme of sexuality runs from the beginning of scripture to the end, it means that our first task is to discover the hermeneutic of the whole before examining particular passages.

Some of you reading this book may like to put puzzles together. Everyone I know who does this always keeps the box top on the table where all the pieces are scattered. The box top guides the identification and placement of each piece. The box top tells us that blue pieces belong to the sky, green pieces to grass, and so on. By looking at the big picture, we learn where the little pieces go. And so it is with the study of scripture.

It dawned on me that I had not been doing this, looking at the whole, and I saw that most of the books about a biblical theology of sexuality had not done it either. Almost all began with five or six passages and tried to "work their way up" to a biblical message. This is backward, a reversal of the first principle in inductive Bible study. The first task is to discover the overarching hermeneutic and then use it to study the parts. The rest of this chapter is a description of the overall hermeneutic, what I call a hermeneutic of covenant love.[5] I developed this hermeneutic by using six vantage points of biblical revelation, and their combined message is the foundation of the theology of sexuality I am describing in this book.

Creator

All bona fide theology begins with God. We understand who we are and how we are supposed to live by looking at who God is and how God acts. We do this because we are made in the image of God, and we can be "like God" inwardly and outwardly in our humanity. Eugene Peterson nails down the God core in these words: "First God. God is the subject of life. God is foundational for living. If we don't have a sense of the primacy of God, we will never get it right, get life right, get our lives right. Not God at the margins; not God as an option; not God on the weekends. God at the center and circumference; God first and last; God, God,

God."[6] His words are consistent with what William Temple wrote a generation earlier: the more our concept of God is wrong, the more dangerous we are to ourselves and others.[7]

With respect to human sexuality, we have largely failed to heed the counsel of Temple and Peterson. We have too much rooted our theology of sexuality in a view of God that is punitive and retributive, and we have too often made anthropology (who we are) a starting point more than theology (who God is). A hermeneutic of love requires that we make God central. We begin to recover that centrality by noting the name most often given to God in the Bible—YHWH. The main attributes of God are discernable in relation to that name: merciful, gracious, faithful, forgiving, and steadfast (or loyal) in love.[8] From YHWH we get the panoramic view of God's disposition toward everyone and everything. In the final dimension—faithful love—we are taken into the heart of God.

The foundational revelation of God in the Bible is that God is love (1 John 4:18). Far from being a view based on a single verse, it is the culmination of scriptural revelation, particularly expressed over and over in the words *hesed* and *agape.* This understanding, that God is love, gives the Bible its coherence, and it is the starting point for developing a biblical theology of human sexuality.

We see that *hesed* and *agape* reveal how God's love is offered to all, without qualification (e.g., Jer 32:24a; John 3:16). It is overflowing and never ending. This love is sacred, faithful, and permanent. God's love alone is enough to move us to wonder and worship. But as we explore God's love, we find that ancient words are also used to describe the kind of love we can experience and

14

share. Indeed, when the love of God is shed abroad in our hearts, we love like God loves! This is grace and truth.

Creation

It stands to reason that there would be congruence between the creator and the creation. David wrote of it this way: "Heaven is declaring God's glory; the sky is proclaiming his handiwork" (Ps 19:1). The creation is the revelation of God, who is love. Gregory of Nyssa saw creation as the script of that revelation.[10] Bernard of Clairvaux wrote extensively about it in his books *The Love of God* and *Song of Songs*. Francis and his followers celebrated the natural order, thinking of it as the first Bible.[11] Julian of Norwich summed it up: "Everything has being by the love of God."[12]

But lest we think that the love connection between the creator and the creation is an ancient thing, we need only turn to the writings of paleontologist and priest Pierre Teilhard de Chardin. He summed up his scientific/theological synthesis by writing, "The physical structure of the universe is love."[13] He described love as the energy pulsating throughout the cosmos from the smallest particle to the farthest star. He saw this especially in the essential oneness of creation, the power of attraction, and the impulse toward transcendence. Louis Savary, who studied Teilhard's theology of love extensively, provides this helpful summary: "The creation of the universe is the primary act of God's self-expression and an important part of God's self-revelation to us."[14] Richard Rohr brings it all together by writing, "Everything visible, without exception, is the outpouring of God."[15] In short, we come from love, we live in love, and we are moving toward love—all because of who God is and how God has made all things.

Many scientific insights about creation are greatly informing our theology, which is one reason why a theological position takes into account what we are discovering from tradition, reason, and experience.[16] We now turn to the Bible itself to see how our scientific understanding of creation provides key input for a theology of sexuality. When we do so, there are at least four things to note.

First, creation is nonbinary.[17] I am using the term *nonbinary* because the aim of this book is to explore sexuality, and *nonbinary* is the word used most often to speak of gender and identity. The idea of nonbinary humanity is itself the result of a larger view of creation often described as nondual.

The essential oneness of creation is understood through the lens of quantum physics, where we now understand that the entire cosmos is a unit—everything is connected—but the one cosmos includes incalculable diversity.[18] This quantum knowledge of the universe is expanded and strengthened by an understanding of light, which is itself one, but with variety that's visible when it's passed through a prism.[19] Our awareness of a loving God is also illuminated by divine light: "God is light, and there is no darkness in him at all" (1 John 1:5).

While the first creation story in the Bible, Genesis 1:1–2:4, is a liturgical narrative in praise of God's generative work over six days, it celebrates the nondual/nonbinary creation of all things. There are pairings in the story—heavens/earth, night/day, and land/sea—but none of the pairings is a doublet. Every pairing is a spectrum within which a variety of expressions occur. For

16

example, in the night/day pairing there is dawn, early morning, midmorning, noon, early afternoon, midafternoon, early evening, evening, night, midnight, and more night—before the whole cycle starts over again. Night and day are a biblical pairing, but they are not a doublet. Every other pairing in the creation story is also a spectrum metaphor, not a binary one.[20] We live in a cosmos that is marvelously varied. The writer of Genesis saw this and celebrated it on the Sabbath.

The arrangement of creation in a nondual/nonbinary fashion emerges from a source prior to the creation: the nature of God as Trinity, which is an essential oneness that makes room for diversity. The God we know and worship is three in one. So it is not surprising that what is made would be congruent with the maker. The cosmos is a mirror of its creator. Richard Rohr describes it this way: "The inner life of the Trinity has become the outer life of all creation. . . . If a loving Creator started this whole thing, then there has to be a 'DNA connection,' as it were, between the One who creates and what is created."[21]

With this revelation of diversity from the biblical text itself, and from related theological interpretation of the scripture, it's amazing that when the writer of the first creation story describes the male/female pairing, some theologians insist that it is only a doublet, a two.[22] This assumption is inconsistent with all the other pairings from the creation narrative in praise of the creator. It also runs counter to the understanding of humanity, which the natural and behavioral sciences are revealing today.[23] The pairings are spectrum categories, not twos. Everything that exists does so in a nonbinary fashion. All means all.

17

Second, creation of the species. We see evidence of species in the biblical word translated as *kind.* The Hebrew word *miyn* is most nearly what we mean today when we speak of species. By using the word *kind,* we may easily think of the word as singular, and that would be accurate if by that we mean singularity—that is, arising from a common oneness. But the Genesis writer uses it more than once, and uses it to describe a variety of things created "each according to its kind"—the Bible's way of acknowledging diversity. But how many species are we talking about? Most scientists say it's impossible to know for sure because species are simultaneously dying out and being discovered. But when pressed, a number of 8.7 million emerges as a reasonable estimate.[24]

We know this by observation. Think of the many kinds of flowers we are describing when we use the word *flower.* Then, put any other word on the table—fish, dog, vegetable. Every "kind" is simultaneously a one and a many. Why would we think it would be any different when we come to *humankind?* The combination of a pervasive nonbinary creation with the biblical idea of kind makes it difficult to imagine that we would develop a theology where the word *two* defines humanity. But that is the polarizing message we have been given by defenders of an "either/or" exclusionary Christianity. The problem is that a binary interpretation does not arise from the creation story itself. Rather, we see the message of species, with the additional use of plural words to describe what God was making: waters, plants, seeds, trees, lights, stars, birds, animals, livestock, crawling things, and wildlife (see Gen 1:6-25). The ontological message is one of plurality, diversity, and variety—at work in every aspect of creation. Humanity is no different. The writer of the first creation story ends the account saying that "God completed all the work that he had done" (Gen 2:2). All means all.

Third, the creation narrative is a liturgical moral insight. The creation story is not only about ontology but also about morality. The core word for this is *good.*[25] The word is used seven times in the first creation story, with the phrase "very good" used at the end of the creation process. When something is good, it is inherently valuable, contributive to the whole (as in the sense of fit and purpose), beautiful to behold, and morally righteous. This is the way God viewed the entirety of creation. God was pleased with everyone and everything, God blessed everyone and everything. All means all.

Within the idea of goodness we find a very important notion. In theological language it is called original righteousness, the story revealed in the pre-fall narrative that we read in Genesis 1 and 2. Unfortunately, some begin their interpretation of sexuality by using the story of the fall in Genesis 3 to allege that an LGBTQ identity is an expression of the fall. But that is reading something into the text, not what the text itself says. Of course, our sexuality is fallen, like everything else, but there is no basis for alleging that this pertains to sexual identity. That assumption is made in relation to a binary (male/female, heterosexual) view of creation—a view shown above to be inaccurate. The Bible more nearly defines sexual fallenness in terms of unfaithful behavior (e.g., sexual immorality and adultery), not identity. In fact, to allege that an LGBTQ identity is a distortion of God's creation is one of the key misinterpretations that lead LGBTQ people to believe they are somehow less than fully human. From that conclusion about subhuman identity, individuals are driven to do harm to themselves through dangerous behaviors and even to the point of taking their own lives.[26]

Instead of imposing a conclusion about fallen nature, we begin to do theology where the story begins in Genesis 1–2, with original righteousness, not original sin. This starting point is one of the keynotes in a biblical Wesleyan theology, and with respect to sexuality it is essential to nail down goodness before we hammer any kind of fallenness. Original righteousness is where we must begin.[27]

Fourth, the image of God. The preceding three insights reach their apex in the fourth element we see in the creation, that we are made in the image of God (Gen 1:26-28), in the likeness of God. It is from this reality that we get a theology of godliness. God has made everyone to be akin in human nature to what God is in divine nature. And in keeping with the three preceding points, all means all. By virtue of being made in the image of God we have the capacity to enter a relationship with God, a lover/beloved relationship. Thomas Merton described it this way: "To say that I am made in the image of God is to say that love is the reason for my existence, for God is love. Love is my true identity. Love is my true character. Love is my name."[28] This is the message the creator sends to us through the creation.

Covenant

In the same way that the creation reflects the creator, the covenant reveals the will of the creator for the creation. The covenant adds the word *life* to the love and light we have already seen in the nature and activity of God, putting into words how holy living is meant to be expressed on a day-to-day basis. The God of Life intends for us to live! Twice in Deuteronomy we read that the covenant was given so that we might live (4:1; 30:19). Jesus, in turn, declared "life to the fullest" to be his mission (John 10:10).

God's invitation to life through the covenant is an invitation to all. When God gave the covenant to Noah, it was to be a covenant with "every living being" (Gen 9:10). When that universal covenant was reaffirmed to Abraham, it was to be a covenant with "all the families of the earth" (12:3). In this second installment, Israel receives its commission to be a light to the nations, not merely for themselves.[29] To make it even clearer, God said that covenant love is to be shown as much to refugees and immigrants as to Israelites (Lev 19:33-34 and Deut 10:17-19). Indeed, Israel's call was to be a light to the nations, shedding and sharing the two great commandments: the love of God (Deut 6:4) and the love of neighbor (Lev 19:18). Idolatry stopped the first sharing; selfishness stopped the second. But from the moment the commission was given, it was intended to be one of covenant love. Walter Brueggemann describes covenant love as Israel's credo.[30]

The covenant is multifaceted and greatly detailed, as a way of showing that God is not only concerned about the totality of our lives, but also that God is active in all the details, providing grace and guidance. The distinction between sacred and secular disappears as the Spirit of God blows across the whole of creation. In that divine breath we discern four characteristics of the covenant: sacredness (holiness), fidelity (faithfulness), and permanency (unending). The idea of monogamy (singular devotion) is also present, and when we look at sexuality in relation to covenant love, this fourth element comes into play as well, especially with the coming of the new covenant. The life God wills and provides for us is characterized by sacredness, fidelity, permanency, and monogamy.

Through these four character-forming commitments of covenant love we see how the goodness of creation becomes operative. Life is good when all four commitments define and direct us. This formation shapes our sexuality as well. From these values we see that the morality of sexuality is not determined by a person's gender, identity, or orientation but rather by honoring the commitments of the covenant. And because the covenant is universal, the possibility of sexual righteousness exists for everyone, just as the potential for sexual sin does. Holy sexuality is possible for all people; there is one standard of righteousness. I call it affirmative accountability.

Affirmative accountability describes all the ways we keep the covenant with respect to sexuality. It also calls out two artificial impositions currently placed on LGBTQ people.

First, the allegation that LGBTQ people must be celibate for life. There is nothing in the biblical understanding of covenant that requires lifelong celibacy for anyone. Celibacy in the Old and New Testaments is a voluntary lifestyle chosen by the person, not one imposed on the person.[31] For Christians, to require lifelong celibacy of LGBTQ people is to demand something that the Bible does not require. Yet this is precisely what some Christians do, usually within the mindset of a welcoming but not affirming perspective.

Second, the prohibition of marriage. Again, there is nothing in the biblical covenant that specifically prohibits same-sex marriage.[32] Marriage is not defined by gender but by the covenantal values of sacredness, fidelity, permanency, and monogamy.[33] This is one reason why marriage is referred to as a holy covenant. Any two people can make solemn promises that declare their intention to live together in ways that honor and reflect sacredness (holiness), fidelity (faithfulness), and permanency (unending). There is nothing in the scriptural interpretation of covenant that permits marriage for heterosexual people but denies it for LGBTQ people.[34]

Much more could be said about the role of covenant in the development of a theology of sexuality, but we see clearly that covenant defines holy sexuality and directs how it is to be expressed. Essentially, the covenant is an affirmation of inclusion—available to all and livable by all.[35] That some Christians fail to see or refuse to acknowledge this has led to many of the current misinterpretations of sexuality, and it contributes to much of the harm done to LGBTQ persons through the views and prohibitions leveled against them, in the name of God, and with a "the Bible tells me so" attitude—when neither God nor the Bible has anything to do with the fear or disapproval of the other.

Christ

As with everything else, when we come to Christ, we come to the apex of our theological hermeneutic. The excarnate and incarnate Christ is the lens through whom we see the revelation of God for eternity and within time.[36] In the excarnate Christ, we see the

23

roughly 13.7 billion years of the Christ presence in the creation we can observe, what the apostle John referred to as the Word (John 1). In the incarnate Christ, we see the thirty-three-year life of Jesus of Nazareth, whom John called the Word made flesh. In Christ we see the revelations of universality and particularity, which enable us to recognize and respond to God now and forever.

Within the context of sexuality, Paul offers a way to organize this section of the book, "Christ is all things and in all people" (Col 3:11). E. Stanley Jones wrote that "nothing in all literature can compare with this."[37] Both phrases within the sentence make key contributions to a theology of sexuality. When we say that "Christ is all," we carry forward everything previously noted in the name YHWH. That is why the most astounding (and controversial) affirmation of the first Christians was, "Jesus is Lord." This put them on a collision course with Judaism and Rome. But it was their bedrock conviction, one they took from Jesus himself, who said "I and the Father are one" (John 10:30) and "Whoever has seen me has seen the Father" (John 14:9). This conviction reached its peak when the risen Christ told John, "I am the Alpha and the Omega" (Rev 1:8, 22:13). When we say that "Christ is in all," we confirm the revelation of creation.

Saint Athanasius is often quoted to show that this cosmic (excarnate/incarnate) view was foundational in early Christianity: "God was consistent in working through one man to reveal himself everywhere, as well as through the other parts of his creation, so that nothing was left devoid of his Divinity and his self-knowledge...so that the whole universe was filled with the knowledge of the Lord as the waters fill the sea."[38] The revelation of the cosmic Christ, and comments like this from theologians writing about him, are filled with mystery and majesty. But in the context of sexuality, it means what John said:

> Everything came into being through the Word,
> and without the Word
> nothing came into being.
> What came into being
> through the Word was life,
> and the life was the light for all people. (John 1:3-4)

Paul said the same thing:

> All things were created by him:
> both in the heavens and the earth,
> the things that are visible and the things that are invisible.
> Whether they are thrones or powers,
> or rulers or authorities,
> all things were created through him and for him. (Col 1:16)[39]

All means all.

By turning to look at the incarnate Christ, the same story continues. Jesus's ministry was for all (John 12:32) and to all (Matt 11:28). He was on solid ground until . . . until . . . he applied this to the "least of these"—not the least in sacred worth but in what the Old Testament called the "little ones" (*anawim*)—those who had been ignored, marginalized, shunned, and deemed less than by political and religious leaders. Jesus was never more counterintuitive or countercultural than in designing his ministry to be one of going about doing good (note the word *good*) to everyone. It began with his inauguration sermon in Nazareth when he read from Isaiah 61:1-2, but closed the scroll without reading the last line where the prophet spoke about the day of vengeance. He left that out! By omitting the note of vengeance, he was saying that from the outset, his ministry would not be one achieved by retribution but through restoration. The images in the earlier lines that he did read are of delivering good news to the poor, binding up the brokenhearted, releasing the captives, liberating the prisoners, and declaring the Lord's favor.[40] From the outset, Jesus declared his ministry would be for all.

By applying Jesus's wide embrace for all to sexuality, we see him including everyone in two key ways: his blessing of marriage and his acknowledgment of eunuchs (Matt 19:1-12). Jesus's words about marriage are in response to a question about divorce; his response must be kept in that context. In making his response, he affirmed all four components of covenant love: sacredness, fidelity, permanency, and monogamy. What we have seen in the old covenant will continue in the new covenant—which is another way to show that marriage is defined by covenant, not by gender.

Proponents of a "one man/one woman" definition of marriage base that definition on two assumptions: heteronormativity and a (false) equation between the ideas of normativity and definitiveness. We have already shown that in creation theology, heteronormativity (i.e., binary creation) is not upheld, but is rather a spectrum in which male/female is a pairing but not merely a two or a doublet. The second mistake flows from this: the allegation that the Bible defines marriage solely as a "one man/one woman" experience. This falsely blends the notions of normativeness and definitiveness. There are many things that are normative but not definitive. Marriage is one of them.

I grew up in Haskell, Texas. The school district was large enough for us to play eleven-man football. In fact, we had an A team and a B team. Each Thursday and Friday night the stadium lights were on and football was played. But less than twenty miles down the road, there were three other schools whose enrollments limited them to playing six-man football. Each week, their lights were on, and football was being played there too. Football was the game for every school, but there were different expressions of it. Eleven-man football was (and still is) normative, but it has never been definitive. Football is defined by rules that apply to the nature of the game, not the number of players.

And so too with marriage. As I previously pointed out, marriage is defined by covenant, not by gender. The fact that Jesus refers to it in Matthew 19:5 by using "man/woman" language is simply his acknowledgement of the norm for marriage in his day—indeed, for any day. But his definition is covenantal, in which he defines marriage as a relationship that has an indissoluble bond. That's what was missing in much marriage in Jesus's day; it had ceased to be a holy bond and had become a paper contract. Thus marriage was not manifesting the covenant love of sacredness, fidelity, permanency, and monogamy. Jesus's teaching on marriage is about a restoration of covenant, not about a necessary "male/female" expression of it.

This is further confirmed in his use of the term "one flesh." Mistakenly, some Christians turn this metaphor into a physical term. Here, as in other parts of the New Testament, the term for flesh (*sarx*) is a metaphor for a kinship bond, which is not sexual in its essence and is not reserved for a male/female relationship.[41]

27

The flesh-and-bone description is what we today call "being joined at the hip," another way of describing deep and lasting relationships that are not physical in their essence. So, in both speaking of marriage in a covenantal way and as a kinship bond, Jesus acknowledges a "man/woman" marriage, but we jump to a preconceived conclusion (a pretext) if we think Jesus defined marriage solely in that configuration.

Following on the heels of this statement about divorce is Jesus's mention of eunuchs (Matt 19:12). Whether he made these remarks immediately after talking about marriage, or whether Matthew placed his words here, it doesn't matter. Either way, it is a biblical way of showing that sexuality in general is not solely defined in male/female language. His inclusion of eunuchs was Jesus's way of acknowledging sexual diversity, pointing to people whom we today refer to as intersex.[42] Jesus would also have known about homosexual people, but he said nothing about them.[43] When we combine the three things Jesus said in this passage (marriage defined by covenant, marriage as a deep kinship bond, and the reality of sexual diversity), we see in his life and ministry a continuation of the Old Testament's inclusive sexual theology, one that honors sexuality beyond a male/female identity, and one that acknowledges that any two people can honor the principles of covenant love in marriage.

Church

That the church would necessarily extend the development of Christ's theology of sexuality is evident both in its expression as the body of Christ (1 Cor 12:27) and in its mission to take the gospel of Christ into all the world (Acts 1:8). With respect to the first element, we can see the first Christians continuing the ministry of Jesus in its inclusivity—the most radical expression being its inclusion of Gentiles (a process that unfolds in Acts 10–15). The message of universality—which comes through the nature of the creator, the creation, the covenant, and the Christ—is now manifested in the church. All means all.

Paul chose to declare this reality in his letter to the Galatians. He did so by using a prayer that many Jewish men prayed at the start of each day. They gave thanks to God that they were neither Gentiles, slaves, nor women. And with their male superiority intact through a distorted theology, they moved into their day to live allegedly holy lives. But Paul, formerly a Pharisee, saw through the pietistic façade and would have none of it. Instead, he wrote that if anyone intended to live a Christian life, they would understand that through their baptism they had clothed themselves with Christ. They have an identity and a perspective in which "there is neither Jew nor Greek; there is neither slave nor free; nor is there male and female, for you are all one in Christ Jesus" (Gal 3:28). This was a watershed statement for anyone; it would have been a blockbuster for any male who had moved, or intended to move, from Judaism into Christianity. It was the clearest way Paul ever expressed inclusivity (he did it in other writing too and against the backdrop of Gentile inclusion), and it was a sign of living in the Spirit rather than in the flesh. E. Stanley Jones commented on this by showing that in this one sentence Paul "sweeps the field" of every distinction: racial, religious, cultural, economic, social, and sex (gender), concluding that "nothing could be more thorough-going."[44] All means all.

Despite the radical inclusivity of Paul's statement, some Christians try to sidestep the message by saying, "But Paul did not include LGBTQ people in his statement." This fragile attempt is proven false in two ways. First, Paul was using a Jewish prayer to make his point. So, his response was intentionally framed to show that the prayer was a counterfeit spirituality, not holiness. And second, Paul added the last phrase "you are all one in Christ Jesus" as his fill-in-the-blank inclusion, saying in effect, "Add anyone else to this list. Any questions?"

If this revelation is not enough, consider Luke's story about the conversion of the Ethiopian eunuch (Acts 8:26-39). No one reading Luke's account would have missed the fact that the first named convert outside Israel was a sexual minority—the same person whom Jesus had used to affirm sexual diversity in Matthew 19. So the biblical witness of the church does, in fact, add sexual diversity in its list of those who are "one in Christ Jesus." People of other than heterosexual identity are not distortions of God's original design; they are not defective human beings. There is no attempt to "pray the gay away" or have them first undergo "conversion therapy" in order to be accepted in the body of Christ. They are not relegated to the status of second-class Christians, welcomed to attend church but not have access to its ministries (e.g., baptism, marriage, and ordination) or to roles of leadership. In scripture, LGBTQ people are one with everyone else in human nature, and they are one with every other Christian through their profession of faith in Jesus Christ. This is the witness of the church. All means all.

Consummation

The final component of our hermeneutic is to see how what takes place in time plays out in eternity. Before the close of the New Testament, Christians are speaking of life in Christ as a new creation (2 Cor 5:17). The writer of Hebrews speaks of it as a new covenant, one written on the heart, not on tablets of stone. The incarnate Christ has initiated all of this: the already/not yet reality of the kingdom of God is in motion. Christians living to the close of the New Testament (and those of us who have lived since) are in the time between the times, where we do not yet see all things in subjection to Christ, but we do see him (Heb 2:8). And before the end of the Bible, we see him once again as the excarnate Christ, who declares himself to be the Alpha and the Omega. Through John's encounter with the cosmic Christ, we are given a glimpse of how all this culminates in a new heaven and a new earth.

Not surprisingly, the consummation of all things is a picture of what we have seen here on earth. In the Lord's Prayer, we pray "on earth as it is in heaven," but now in the book of Revelation we see "in heaven as it has been on earth." John describes the scene in these words: "I looked, and there was a great crowd that no one could number. They were from every nation, tribe, people, and language. They were standing before the throne and before the Lamb" (Rev 7:9). This is the ultimate revelation that all means all.

31

And what we see is the consummation of the trajectory that has been in place before the creation of the world, the plan in mind all along that's made real and ultimate in Christ—the consummation of love. Paul says of it, "God revealed his hidden design [or mystery] to us, which is according to his goodwill and the plan that he intended to accomplish through his Son. This is what God planned for the climax of all times [fullness of time]: to bring all things together in Christ, the things in heaven along with the things on earth" (Eph 1:9-10).

What we see in John's vision has been the plan all along, what Luke referred to as "the restoration of all things" (Acts 3:21). Of course, this is *mystery*! But it is the Bible's way of describing the deepest possible *reality*.

This is the hermeneutic for interpreting what the Bible says about intimate human sexuality; it is a hermeneutic of love. We see it in the creator, the creation, the covenant, the Christ, the church, and the consummation. It is the message of total and radical oneness, similar to Jesus's hope in his prayer in John 17. In the context of sexuality, it means all persons are holy and can live holy lives that include the holy love of sexual expression. No one is a distortion; no one is defective. We are all made in the image of God. We are all included. We are all affirmed. We are all given full access to everything God has to offer: no exceptions. Of course, we are accountable—every one of us—to live as God's beloved, as those who seek to honor the covenant, as those who desire to be Christlike, as those who want to be members of the church with access to all its means of grace and ministries, and as those who envision the day when we will stand around the throne of the Lamb. It is, in short, an invitation offered to everyone—an invitation that resonates in our deepest self, evoking a grand "Yes, I accept. For this I am made!"

This is the hermeneutic that has transformed my theology of sexuality. It is the hermeneutic of love that I believe is the essence and foundation of all living Christian faith. It is the hermeneutic I hope to share to my dying day—summed up in three glorious words: all means all!

Discussion

1. When you read the phrase "a hermeneutic of love," what words or images come to your mind? How is love interpreted by your personal experience?

2. Which of the six *C*s (creator, creation, covenant, Christ, church, consummation) meant the most to you. Why?

3. Do any of the six *C*s call you to further reflection and study? Why?

4. Do you agree that a theology of love (that is, "God is love") is a key to interpreting what the Bible says about sexuality? Why or Why not?

THREE

THE PASSAGES

With covenant love understood, we are in a position to explore specific scriptural passages. With many books and articles, that has meant moving immediately to the five passages used to make a case against same-sex relationships. LGBTQ people rightly refer to these passages as "clobber" texts. But that is not where we will go next, and that is again because of a principle from inductive methodology—every passage has a backdrop or wider context that enables us to interpret it more accurately. With respect to sexuality, that backdrop is found in two important revelations: the stories of love in the Bible, and the broad range of admonitions that grant permission and prohibition.

From the garden of Eden to the new heaven and new earth, love stories abound in scripture. In the Old Testament we see peaks of insight into the relationships between God and human beings, and between couples who lead the advance of the people of God across land and time—relationships that reach a climax in the Song of Songs. In the New Testament, our reading begins with the greatest love story ever told (John 3:16), the revelation of incarnate love in Jesus (John 13:1), the manifesto of love (1 Cor 13), the

35

mystery of marriage as an analogy of the love between Christ and the church (Eph 5:21-33), and the marriage of Christ and the Bride in heaven (Rev 21:2).[1]

Before we look at any particular passage about sexuality, we need to study and ponder the sweep of the love stories we find in the Bible. We need to note the characteristics of those relationships and use them as further enhancements to the hermeneutic of covenant love. When we do this, we discover that sexuality in scripture is more than physical activity. Sexuality is an energy before it is an expression. Human beings are not essentially sexual because they engage in sexual activity but because we are created with the strong desire for relationships. The revelation of scripture is a picture of sexuality that is larger than the physical expressions of it.[2] As with everything else, the source for this understanding is in the nature of God, who creates without physical activity. Creativity is an energy that gives rise to other things. The energy is described in the Trinity as a divine dance (*perichoresis*) in which relationships are primary and life is the outcome of the interaction. Scientists now see this same dance going on between the smallest particles and the largest galaxies through laws of synchronicity—interactions that create, attract, and sustain life at every level.

Before we ever get to sexuality as physicality, we dwell in the holy land of relationships that exist in a myriad of ways—relationships between people and other people, relationships between people and nature, and relationships between people and God. These relationships are intense and ongoing without ever having to be physical. This is where we derive the idea of chastity, a word greatly limited when it is only linked with refraining from sexual activity. It is more largely the cultivation of single-minded devotion given to someone or to something. In the Bible we see this larger meaning in Paul's use of the word in 2 Corinthians 6:6 and 11:3.[3] We see this kind of commitment in artists, athletes, scientists, educators, homemakers, monks, nuns—indeed, in anyone who brings wholehearted devotion to a relationship. The love stories in the Bible are important in rescuing sexuality from any limitation of it to physical activity. We need this liberation in our day because sexuality is too narrowly understood in that way.

The second backdrop for our study of selected Bible passages that are focused on same-sex behaviors is the plethora of passages that refer to heterosexual behaviors. For some reason, many Christians never get around to mentioning that we have five passages about same-sex sexuality and hundreds about opposite-sex sexuality. By focusing on five passages, we become conditioned to think that the Bible's concern is weighted toward LGBTQ misconduct, when that is simply not the case. Nor is the reality we are dealing with in the church and society today. Sexual misconduct is markedly more prevalent among heterosexuals than homosexuals. We only have to stop and think about this for a moment, and it becomes evident. But by focusing on LGBTQ sexuality, heterosexual conduct is a reality that never seems to make it to our conversations.[4] By focusing on LGBTQ sexuality, we have essentially created a cover-up for the much larger problem of heterosexual sinfulness. The Bible doesn't do that. It puts the weight of evidence where it belongs—on opposite-sex activity, where the potential for sin and abuse was greater in that day and continues to be now. God's concern for sexual sin for all people gets lost when some Christians make LGBTQ sexuality such an emphasis that existing heterosexual sin is never mentioned, and even covered up. When we read the five prohibitions of same-sex behavior that are sinful, we can keep what the Bible says about it in this larger context.

Against the backdrop of the Bible's love stories and its concern for sexual sin throughout the human family, we can look at the five passages cited to make a case against LGBTQ sexuality. Before doing so, it is necessary to point out that there is no consensus among scholars about what these passages are against. Conservatives misrepresent reality and consensus when they allege that their nonaffirming interpretation is the only valid one. It simply is not.[5]

Scholars are not of one mind, which means that both traditional and progressive interpreters are obliged to express descriptions and opinions with charity. So the aim in interpreting the following passages must be to provide a plausible case. Through personal study, using inductive methodology and connecting that study with credible secondary scholarship, I am presenting a plausible interpretation. Whether it is the one you hold or becomes persuasive in leading you to change your mind about these passages, is another matter. I can only bear witness to the fact that the following interpretation has become persuasive for me and for millions of other Christians who believe in the inspiration and authority of scripture as much as any nonaffirming Christian does.

Leviticus 18:22, 20:13

You must not have sexual intercourse [*mishakabe*, "be sleeping around"] with a man as you would with a woman; it is a detestable practice. (Lev 18:22 CEB)

You shall not lie [*mishakabe*] with a male as with a woman; it is an abomination. (Lev 18:22 NRSV)

If a man has sexual intercourse [*mishakabe*, "is sleeping around"] with a man as he would with a woman, the two of them have done something detestable. They must be executed; their blood is on their own heads. (Lev 20:13 CEB)

If a man lies [*mishakabe*] with a male as with a woman, both of them have committed an abomination; they shall be put to death; their blood is upon them. (Lev 20:13 NRSV)

Specific passages arise to address particular concerns.[6] These two verses are within the larger context of sexual conduct, where God says to the people through Moses, "You must not do things like they are done in the land of Egypt, where you used to live. And you must not do things like they are done in the land of Canaan, where I am bringing you" (Lev 18:3). This admonition reflects the key role that sexuality plays in both reflecting and shaping culture.[7] This was true for the Israelites as well, but the people were to express their sexuality differently. In this section of Leviticus there are numerous examples of such difference, one of which is male same-sex behavior.[8]

But what kind of behavior is prohibited in these verses? The verses themselves provide the answer, and it comes through the Hebrew word *shakab*.[9] The essence of the meaning is promiscuity.

39

The Hebrew word suggests "roaming"—that is, sexual behavior that is temporary, lustful, and without commitment. It is what we often refer to today as "sleeping around." The verses themselves are not about the violators (their orientation) but rather about the violation. The verses are not about a physical aberration (absence of anatomical complimentary), but about the violation of covenant love. The sexual sin described in Leviticus violates all four dimensions of covenant love. It is not sacred, faithful, permanent, or monogamous.[10]

The males mentioned in these two verses are not heterosexual or LGBTQ; they are any men who violate covenant love through promiscuous sexual behavior.[11] Without reference to orientation, Leviticus teaches that the sexuality of the Israelites must not be promiscuous as was the case in Egypt and Canaan.[12] Their sexuality was to honor and reflect covenant love, more as a sign of devotion to God rather than a means to make the land fertile and productive.

1 Corinthians 6:9-10; 1 Timothy 1:10

Don't you know that people who are unjust won't inherit God's kingdom? Don't be deceived. Those who are sexually immoral [*pornoi*], those who worship false gods, adulterers [*moikoi*], both participants in same-sex intercourse [*malakoi* or "sexual addicts"], thieves, the greedy, drunks, abusive people, and swindlers won't inherit God's kingdom. (1 Cor 6:9-10 CEB)

Do you not know that wrongdoers will not inherit the kingdom of God? Do not be deceived! Fornicators [*pornoi*], idolaters, adulterers [*moikoi*], male prostitutes, sodomites [*malakoi* or "sexual addicts"], thieves, the greedy, drunkards, revilers, robbers—none of these will inherit the kingdom of God. (1 Cor 6:9-10 NRSV)

They are people who are sexually unfaithful [*pornois*], and people who have intercourse with the same sex [*arsenokoitai* or "sexual abusers"]. They are kidnappers, liars, individuals who give false testimonies in court, and those who do anything else that is opposed to sound teaching. (1 Tim 1:10 CEB)

...fornicators [*pornois*], sodomites [*arsenokoitai* or "sexual abusers"], slave traders, liars, perjurers, and whatever else is contrary to the sound teaching. (1 Tim 1:10 NRSV)

When Paul arrived in Corinth, he was separated by millennia and miles from Canaan, but he encountered aberrant sexual behavior that had to be called out.[13] His lists include two specific types: addiction and abuse. Sexual addiction is seen through the Greek word *malakoi,* and abuse is seen through the word *arsenokoitai.*

By all accounts, both words are rare and difficult to translate. Part of the reason for this lies in the infrequency of both words in scripture, and due to a range of interpretations taken from cultural and religious uses in Greco-Roman culture. In fact, *malakoi* is only used in this passage in the entire Bible. So we must look at extrabiblical materials in order to have any idea what Paul might have had in mind when he wrote to the Corinthians.

Malakoi in the Greco-Roman world is an often-used word to describe unbridled lust. Lust is bad enough, but the people referred to as *malakoi* go beyond lustfulness to something even stronger: sexual addiction. These are people enslaved to passion, who lost all resistance to the power of pleasure; hence, the association of it with addictive behavior. The idea of "softness" attributed to the word is as much an indication of the absence of boundaries as it is to the personalities of the men who lived "soft" lives.[14] *Malakoi* are people whose sexuality is out of control, practiced

41

without respect to people or to boundaries.[15] William Barclay refers to them as sensualists.[16] They are self-indulgent people, to the extreme.

But there's more, because the word *malakoi* described behaviors other than sexual: greed, living in luxurious excess, which generally referred to womanizers, not to same-sex behavior. *Malakoi* were males who seduced women without hesitation and did so over and over. Clearly none of these were LGBTQ people, but even when there was same-sex excess, it was not interpreted as related to a person's orientation but rather to one's being out of control—something that could happen to anyone, something that always violated covenant love. So the people who are *malakoi* break all four dimensions of covenant. Their sexual behavior is not sacred. It is not faithful, permanent, or monogamous.

Paul's second word is *arsenokoitai*. Here we move from addiction to abuse. The word includes self-abuse, but it also refers to the abuse of others—what we would call today sexual exploitation or treating people like objects. In Greco-Roman culture, this was male sexual activity (irrespective of orientation) that usually meant some form of prostitution or pederasty or sex between masters and slaves.[17] And like the word *malakoi,* it was behavior not limited to sexuality but applicable to other areas of life as well. The Sibylline Oracles use the word to describe thievery, betraying a confidence, murder, paying unjust wages to workers, and oppressing the poor.[18] In the context of sexuality we would call such people sex abusers, sex offenders, or sexual predators. Clearly again, this kind of sexuality violates all four dimensions of covenant love. It is not sacred, faithful, permanent, or monogamous.

Romans 1:18-32

God's wrath is being revealed from heaven against all the ungodly behavior and the injustice of human beings who silence the truth with injustice. This is because what is known about God should be plain to them because God made it plain to them. Ever since the creation of the world, God's invisible qualities—God's eternal power and divine nature—have been clearly seen, because they are understood through the things God has made. So humans are without excuse. Although they knew God, they didn't honor God as God or thank him. Instead, their reasoning became pointless, and their foolish hearts were darkened. While they were claiming to be wise, they made fools of themselves. They exchanged the glory of the immortal God for images that look like mortal humans: birds, animals, and reptiles. So God abandoned them to their hearts' desires, which led to the moral corruption of degrading their own bodies with each other. They traded God's truth for a lie, and they worshipped and served the creation instead of the creator, who is blessed forever. Amen.

That's why God abandoned them to degrading lust. Their females traded natural sexual relations for unnatural sexual relations. Also, in the same way, the males traded natural sexual relations with females, and burned with lust for each other. Males performed shameful actions with males, and they were paid back with the penalty they deserved for their mistake in their own bodies. Since they didn't think it was worthwhile to acknowledge God, God abandoned them to a defective mind to do inappropriate things. So they were filled with all injustice, wicked behavior, greed, and evil behavior. They are full of jealousy, murder, fighting, deception, and malice. They are gossips, they slander people, and they hate God. They are rude and proud, and they brag. They invent ways to be evil, and they are disobedient to their parents. They are without understanding, disloyal, without affection, and without mercy. Though they know God's decision that those who persist in such practices deserve death, they not only keep doing these things but also approve others who practice them. (Rom 1:18-32 CEB)

43

For the wrath of God is revealed from heaven against all ungodliness and wickedness of those who by their wickedness suppress the truth. For what can be known about God is plain to them, because God has shown it to them. Ever since the creation of the world his eternal power and divine nature, invisible though they are, have been understood and seen through the things he has made. So they are without excuse; for though they knew God, they did not honor him as God or give thanks to him, but they became futile in their thinking, and their senseless minds were darkened.

Claiming to be wise, they became fools; and they exchanged the glory of the immortal God for images resembling a mortal human being or birds or four-footed animals or reptiles.

Therefore God gave them up in the lusts of their hearts to impurity, to the degrading of their bodies among themselves, because they exchanged the truth about God for a lie and worshiped and served the creature rather than the Creator, who is blessed forever! Amen.

For this reason God gave them up to degrading passions. Their women exchanged natural intercourse for unnatural, and in the same way also the men, giving up natural intercourse with women, were consumed with passion for one another. Men committed shameless acts with men and received in their own persons the due penalty for their error.

And since they did not see fit to acknowledge God, God gave them up to a debased mind and to things that should not be done. They were filled with every kind of wickedness, evil, covetousness, malice. Full of envy, murder, strife, deceit, craftiness, they are gossips, slanderers, God-haters, insolent, haughty, boastful, inventors of evil, rebellious toward parents, foolish, faithless, heartless, ruthless. They know God's decree, that those who practice such things deserve to die— yet they not only do them but even applaud others who practice them. (Rom 1:18-32 NRSV)

Paul had never been to Rome, but he undoubtedly had contact with people who had been there, and they told him, "What you have found in Corinth is also in Rome." He was probably in

Corinth when he received this word, so everything he had recently written in his letter to the Corinthians was very much alive in his mind.[19] Christian sexuality had to honor and reflect covenant love everywhere, so he wanted to address the matter even before he arrived in the city. As we look at the letter to the Romans in general, and when we turn to the selected passage, some very important things stand out.

First, with respect to the general aim of the letter, Paul is writing to show how the gospel (that is, Jesus the Christ) has brought salvation to the world. Standing along with the book of Hebrews, it is a substantive and sustained theological treatise around which most of Paul's other teachings can be gathered.[20] But as Paul wrote to the Roman Christians, he could not merely declare the victorious life as salvation in Christ. He had to show how it was an abundant life that overcomes counterfeited and caricatured life. From beginning to end, Paul's letter to the Romans is his way of declaring the power of God for the salvation of all.

Paul's comments about sexuality occur in the context of this overall soteriological structure. What he had previously told the Galatians about salvation, "Christ has set us free for freedom" (5:1), was now applied to sexuality as with all other aspects of life. In order to understand what he was saying in these verses, we must look at two keys that unlock the passage, enabling us to read it as the Romans themselves would have.

The first key is the context of idolatry and lust. In keeping with the spirit of Leviticus, Paul knew that sexuality has the power to turn us from the true God to false gods. And that was what was happening in the Roman culture. Paul described it as exchanging "the glory of the immortal God for images that look like humans" (Rom 1:23).[21] But as in Leviticus more than five hundred years earlier, and in Corinth not far away, idolatry was not merely the breaking of one of the ten commandments, it was a deformative act of the will, which set in motion a downward spiral into other sinfulness.

In this passage, the downward spiral expresses itself in twenty-one behaviors, one of which is noncovenantal sexuality.[22] Paul describes it as behavior "which led to the moral corruption of their own bodies with each other" (Rom 1:24). At this point, re-read the paragraphs about the sinfulness described in Leviticus and at Corinth—sinfulness driven by lustful (excessively passionate) idolatry (self-gratification). All that idolatry and lust is going on in Rome.

But beyond the context of lustful idolatry, Paul writes about the kind of behavior it produces. He uses two words to describe it: "exchanged" and "unnatural." These two keywords unlock the meaning of the passage. When Paul writes that men (and women too, in this passage) "exchanged" one form of sexuality for another, it is a word of choice that temporarily abandons, sets aside, and ignores the previous existence. These were people leaving behind their customary sexuality for aberrant sexuality. Their behavior was immoral because it was not who they were in their personhood.

And with that context before us, the interpretation comes rolling in: Paul is talking about heterosexual people! They "exchanged" (abandoned, set aside temporarily) who they were and behaved against their orientation. And that's where the word "unnatural" comes in to further strengthen and confirm who Paul was writing about, and what his concern was.[23] It was (and still is) "unnatural" for the men and women Paul is describing because

46

(using contemporary language) they were heterosexuals engaging in homosexual acts.

As it turns out, this is not a passage about LGBTQ people but about heterosexuals behaving badly! Even John Stott, a non-affirming evangelical, recognized this and wrote about it in his book *Homosexual Partnerships*.[24] What Paul is writing about in this passage is what some refer to as a dispositional violation, a deliberate ignoring of one's heterosexual orientation and acting out of character with it.[25] This means that LGBTQ people were not even on Paul's mind so far as the specifics of this passage are concerned. And as with every previous passage, the sexual sin in Rome is a violation of covenant love. It is not sacred, faithful, permanent, or monogamous.

When we combine what we have seen from all five passages, we are left to conclude that there is sexual sin—and people of all orientations can and do commit it. When we put it all together, we see that the Bible is against sexual sin that is promiscuous, driven by excess passion, and abusive—any sexual behavior that shames others by treating them as objects rather than as people, any sexual behavior that subjugates another person and controls them for one's own self-gratification.

But none of the prohibited behaviors in the passages address LGBTQ sexuality, much less forbid it, because Christian LGBTQ people want to honor covenant love as much as heterosexual Christians do. There is no hidden agenda in the gay community. There is no desire for a double standard. LGBTQ people merely want to be allowed to be who they are, and as we have seen, the biblical hermeneutic says they are (like everyone else) human beings made in the image of God, beloved children of God, invited to access and enjoy all the blessings and benefits of sexuality that any other human being is granted. Christian LGBTQ people want to live the same standard of covenant love as much as anyone else—sexuality that is sacred, faithful, permanent, and monogamous. They want to honor the same theology of affirmative accountability. All means all. The biblical hermeneutic reveals it; the five passages confirm it.

Discussion

1. Did you learn anything new from looking at these passages?

2. How do the passages work to produce your view about what God desires for human sexuality and intimacy?

3. How do these passages enrich the "hermeneutic of love" that you discern from scripture and its impact on your daily life?

FOUR

THE LIFE

The journey I wrote about in chapter 1 led me through scripture to the theology of sexuality I presented in the previous two chapters. But it has been more than an exercise in inductive Bible study that produces learning; it has been an exploration that changed my life. As a theologian in the Wesleyan tradition, this is exactly where it must eventuate, because experience, what Wesley called "practical divinity," is where everything must come; otherwise, we are left with theoretical theology, dangling doctrine, what he called "dead orthodoxy." The past five years have been life-altering and life-enriching years. In order to bring this book to where I want it to end, I must again write of my experience and do so in a way that I hope will be helpful to you.

I must write as an advocate and as an ally, for that is who I am. I am an advocate for LGBTQ people with respect to their civil and ecclesial rights. I am an ally with them in their quest for full inclusion in the church. But I realize that some of you reading this are LGBTQ people, so I have written something for you in appendix A. And I imagine that some of you reading this book are nonaffirming Christians. I have written something for you in appendix B. The rest of this chapter envisions readers who either are or seek to be advocates and allies for LGBTQ people. In the spirit of doing theology in the Wesleyan way, I hope to respond to the question, "How then shall we live?"

First, we must live in relationship with LGBTQ people. I became convinced of this shortly after I wrote *For the Sake of the Bride*. The prologue of this book provides an illustration for this, as will the epilogue. But intellectually, I recognized the importance of this in an interview conducted with Walter Brueggemann.[1] He spoke of how relationships are necessary for creating theological imagination—what he means by turning texts into life. In fact, he spoke about growing weary in trying to persuade others solely through exegetical prowess. When I read his interview and connected it with my emerging experience, I saw the centrality of befriending LGBTQ people. The past five years have proven the correctness, power, and beauty of doing this. Jeannie and I have gotten to know LGBTQ people who are as devoted to Christ as anyone could ever be, and we have been loved and supported by them when other Christians (some friends of longstanding) have gone silent or voiced criticism of us. And so, I must make my first word of counsel to be establishing friendships with LGBTQ people.

Second, we must live as lifelong learners with respect to sexuality. One of the things that has become clear in my study is how some Christians are using outdated information to build their nonaffirming theology. I imagine that many do not realize they are doing this. But I venture that some are not interfacing with new discoveries precisely because they know that doing so would weaken their position. However it happens, it is something we must avoid. I say this from firsthand experience when I began to do my theological homework. I was behind the times. In recognizing this about myself and others, I have come to believe that the ultimate problem in the Christian community with respect to a theology of sexuality is not that we disagree on some things; Christians have done that over and over. The ultimate problem is that some Christians are using data to support their case that is no longer considered credible. Knowingly or unknowingly, they are spreading falsehoods and using theological authority to do it.

One discovery illustrates the point. The allegation that gender identity is fixed at birth and presented anatomically is simply not a fact. Experts in the physical and behavioral sciences are proving that much more is involved.[2] Gender identity is still viewed as essentially hormonal (with identifiable external social factors in play), but scientists now know that the same hormones that create the anatomical differences continue to be active in the brain after birth. Neural variations (in both makeup and connectivity) lead to a person's gender identity, developed variously over time between early childhood and when a person reaches puberty. Because most of this occurs at the genetic level, there is still much to be learned. But we know enough to realize that anatomical presentation at birth is not definitive of gender identity. Christians or politicians who continue to take this position are working with outdated information.

With respect to lifelong learning, I have also realized that I must pay attention to what younger people are saying. There is a generational difference that must not be ignored. Whether we like it or not, those of us who are older have grown up with views about sexuality that younger people do not hold. They have grown up in different contexts than we did, with different relationships than we had, and with a closer connection to current information than we do. To ignore them, or to allege that they are under the influence of fallen-world thinking, is blatantly wrong and uncharitable. On the contrary, what they show us and tell us is essential in developing a theology of sexuality in the present age. So both in terms of our research and our listening to others, we must be lifelong learners with respect to a theology of sexuality.

Third, we must live as nonviolent resisters to those who spread misinformation, and worse, whose words and actions do harm to LGBTQ people. The need for this is as great as at any time in history when people have been marginalized and oppressed. Those who claim they "love the gays" and are not doing harm to them have not formed the friendships I've talked about earlier or taken the time to show up where LGBTQ people are telling their stories. Given my experience, I would say that all you have to do is attend one meeting with LGBTQ people and ask them if they have been harmed by Christians, and you will leave with a truckload of responses, not only from those willing to tell you of the harm they have experienced, and that of others whom they know. If it seems that I am weary of those Christians who attempt to exonerate themselves with an "I love you, but..." view—I am. From the standpoint of experience, nothing has become clearer to me than that some Christians are trying to validate their testimony while insufficiently hearing from LGBTQ persons, who tell a much different story than is alleged by the mantra "we love the gays."[3]

In this accidental or intentional milieu, nonviolent resistance is called for. By realizing this, I had to educate myself through the writings of those who have engaged in nonviolent resistance in the past and continue to do so today. I read Bonhoeffer, Gandhi, Merton, Day, Thurman, Romero, and King, but also those currently engaged in the resistance: John Dear, Jonathan Wilson-Hartgrove, William Barber III, Liz Theoharis, Wil Gafney, and others.[4] Walter Brueggemann has been especially helpful to me in the integration of theology and resistance through his writings about prophetic ministry (in the Bible and in the culture today), emphasizing the threefold task of calling out (naming the evil), calling up (a vision of the good, rooted in covenant love), and calling forth (through concrete actions) people who will be instruments of God's peace in the movement toward shalom—toward the new creation. We must live in the society and in the church as nonviolent resisters against deformative theologies of sexuality and against harmful efforts to denigrate, marginalize, and oppress LGBTQ people.

Fourth, we must live as promoters of access for LGBTQ people into all the church's sacraments, means of grace, and ministries. It is a good thing that many churches have declared themselves publicly as "loving all people." But the time in which we find ourselves mandates that we move beyond affirmation to access. LGBTQ people must not only be permitted to attend church (and of course, give their money) and even be members of it, but they must also be invited to give themselves in ministry within the body of Christ (both lay and ordained), and they must be allowed to marry in the church just as heterosexual people are.

As good as affirmation is, if it is not followed with access, LGBTQ people will see it as another version of "I love you, but…" and they will either move toward other denominations that offer full access or add themselves to the growing list of "dones" so far as believing that the Christian church is for them. One of the things I have seen the past few years is a remarkable patience among LGBTQ people toward the church. But as time goes by, their patience is legitimately wearing thin. If we care, we must be more proactive than ever in advocating full inclusion of LGBTQ people in the church.

Finally, we must live keeping watch over ourselves as advocates and allies. I save this point for last because it is where living faith ends up. Simply put, we must enact the two great commandments and reflect the fruit of the Spirit in our support for LGBTQ people. We must live in love.[5] Whenever we fail to do this, we are no better in character or conduct than those with whom we disagree. We cannot advocate love without practicing it. And I will be the first to confess that I have not always done this. It is easy to get caught up in the moment and deteriorate into attitudes and actions like those with whom we disagree. But whenever passion overtakes perspective, we have lost the place to stand in asserting our views so that they can be heard. This is what Richard Rohr means when he says that "the best criticism of the bad is the practice of the better. Oppositional energy only creates more of the same."[6] It is what Martin Luther King Jr. called "strength to love."[7]

My journey into a new biblical theology of sexuality has been a journey into greater love. But that immersion into scripture has been accompanied by a parallel journey into a deeper understanding of love as the singular mark of the mature Christian life.[8] Love must be the North Star in our theological sky and the anchor in our spirit as we advocate on behalf of LGBTQ people. Ilia Delio has been another valued guide in this journey. Her words capture the essence of how we must live in love: "God invites us to become more whole within ourselves so that we may become more whole among ourselves. Evolution toward greater wholeness is evolution toward more life and love."[9]

Here is the place where everything I have written in this book comes together into an overarching biblical theology of sexuality that is both believed and practiced. It is here where faith becomes life. It is a life that enables us to recognize the challenge Bishop Karen Oliveto writes about: "This much is clear: as long as the lives of LGBTQ persons are reduced to an 'issue,' it is easy to discount the movement of the Holy Spirit in their lives and therefore maintain a status quo that confers 'less than' and second-class status on them."[10] It is the life that moves us to respond with a commitment to be allies of LGBTQ people with nothing less than Isaiah's words, "I'm here; send me."

Discussion

1. Which recommendations in this chapter are you currently embracing? What have you learning by doing so?

2. Which recommendations in this chapter do you hope to enact in the future? What do you hope to learn or gain?

3. What other behaviors or activities came to mind as you read this chapter? Are you already doing some of them? If not, how do intend to begin doing them?

AND SO IT CONTINUES

I saw her as soon as I stood up to speak, seated in the front row but far to the left. From the moment I began my presentation until it ended, her eyes were fixed on me. And when the session was over, she waited to speak with me, but only after everyone else who wanted to had done so.

"Did you read my card?" she asked. We had collected questions and comments on cards so that the discussion time could flow naturally. I hesitated, not having any idea which one would have been hers. I showed her the cards, and she pointed to hers when I came to it. But rather than waiting for me to read it, she began,

> I was kicked out of my home by my parents "in the name of God." I was homeless, depressed, and had nowhere to go. My only friend was a trans fellow who, like me, had been despised and rejected. He took me in. But last week, he took his life, convinced that he was less than human, worthless. Christians had told him so—more than once. I came here tonight hoping I might hear a different message, and I did. But you still did not answer the question that is eating away at me: How can a God of love let this happen? To me? To my friend? How can you say God loves me if Christians call me an abomination and leave me to live a life of loneliness and depression?

I responded the best I could in the moment. But I could tell that my attempts to offer her another picture of God had not taken away the one she had been given—by her parents, by Christians, by the church. She asked me if the church we were in was LGBTQ friendly, and I assured her it was. I asked her if she lived close enough to come back. She answered, "I'd rather not say." And with that, she thanked me for my presentation and for spending some time with her. She turned and walked out of the room.

And so, it continues…

YOU ARE LOVED

I f you identify as an LGBTQ person, I hope this book has encouraged you. You are one of the reasons I wrote it. But before you put it down, I have something more important than this book that I want to write to you. I want you to know that YOU ARE LOVED!

YOU... as you are, made in the image of God (Gen 1:26-28), fearfully and wonderfully made (Ps 139:14), just a little lower than the angels (Ps 8:5). No matter what lies you have been told or how badly you have been treated, you are God's beloved! And as such you are a person of sacred worth, a full and whole member of the human family. Yes, YOU!

ARE... right now, in this moment. Not when you become someone else or act like someone else. God invites you to live fully in the present moment; Jesus offers you abundant life here and now. You do not have to live in fear or in secret, at least not as far as God is concerned. And shame on anyone (including Christians) who have made you believe otherwise. "Now is the day of salvation" (2 Cor 6:2)—where you are and as you are. Today is the day to walk in the light as God is in the light and to do so as an LGBTQ child of the light. You ARE loved.

LOVED...immersed in love, covered in love, drenched in love, embraced by love, kissed by love. That's *hesed* and *agape*. It's the "welcome home" that the father gave to his younger son (Luke 15:11-24). It's full inclusion into the family and full access into the house. No spiritual food is denied you. No room is off limits to you. You're home! You are LOVED!

God is not mad at you; God is madly in love with you. Believe this—it is true!

A WORD TO NONAFFIRMING CHRISTIANS

It is important for you to know that I have not written this book to log a win but to make a witness. I have not written to reveal what I am against but to declare what I am for, and it is this: a bona fide nonconservative biblical theology of sexuality exists—yes, a *biblical* theology. The fact that some nonaffirming Christians act as if theirs is the only legitimate interpretation does not negate the fact that what they hold is only one view; there are others, and mine is one of them—a view shared by many other Christians as well.

It is also important for you to know that I believe in the inspiration and authority of scripture as much as any conservative does. My change of mind with respect to sexuality has not affected my belief in the Bible one bit, nor has it changed my affirmation of faith as per the creeds. I have been treated by some as if I have junked the whole Christian enterprise, but that is simply not true—and thankfully some of my conservative Christian friends know it. They know that I believe the Bible is our foundational authority in matters of faith and practice, that it is our "supreme court" (to borrow Albert Outler's phrase) when it comes to discerning our beliefs and practices. In that context, I have written this book as an orthodox Christian.

And finally, it is important for you to know that I still long for a day when we can talk with each other about all this, not just talk about each other. I tried to make that clear in the "Gathering at the Round Table" chapter in *For the Sake of the Bride.* But time has not brought that hope into reality for the most part. In fact, as I write these words, the divide between conservatives and progressives seems wider than ever, complete with adversarial language that makes reconciliation even more difficult. Nevertheless, I want you to know that I still believe we would all be better off, and in a better place as the church, if we rolled up our sleeves and did the much harder work of holy conferencing.

FOR FURTHER READING

T he following reading list is a relatively short one to take you further into a study of an affirming theology of sexuality. Even though this is a book focusing on scripture, I have intentionally grouped suggested readings to correspond to the Wesleyan quadrilateral. This will take your study into the other dimensions of theological hermeneutics. Most books transcend one category; I have placed each one where it had the most direct influence on my study. In each category you will find a double asterisk—**—that indicates the book I recommend you read first. Additionally, each book has footnotes and bibliographies that will take you even further.

Scripture

Mark Achtemeier, *The Bible's Yes to Same-Sex Marriage*
James Brownson, *Bible, Gender, and Sexuality*
Richard Freeman and Shawna Dolansky, *The Bible Now*
Luke Timothy Johnson, *The Living Gospel* (chapter 8)
Jennifer Knust, *Unprotected Texts*
William Loader, *Sexuality and the New Testament*

Linda Patterson, *Hate Thy Neighbor: How the Bible Is Misused to Condemn Homosexuality*

**Dan Via's section in *Homosexuality and the Bible: Two Views*

Walter Wink, *Homosexuality and the Bible*

Tradition

**Cheryl Anderson, *Ancient Laws and Contemporary Controversies*

John Boswell, *Christianity, Social Tolerance, and Homosexuality*

Francis Mondimore, *A Natural History of Homosexuality*

Reason (Theology and Science)

Theology

**Megan Shanon DeFranza, *Sex Differences in Christian Theology*

Karen Keen, *Scripture, Ethics and the Possibility of Same-Sex Relationships*

Jack David Rogers, *Jesus, the Bible, and Homosexuality* (Revised Edition)

Robert Song, *Covenant and Calling*

Science

Jacques Balthazart, *The Biology of Homosexuality*

Jerold Greenberg, *Exploring Dimensions of Human Sexuality*

Justin Lehmiller, *The Psychology of Human Sexuality*

Simon LeVay, *Gay, Straight and the Reason Why* (Second Edition)

**Michael Regele, *Science, Scripture, and Same-Sex Love*

Experience

**David Gushee, *Changing Our Minds* (Third Edition)

Steve Harper, *For the Sake of the Bride*

James Martin, *Building a Bridge*

Tim Otto, *Oriented to Love*
Matthew Vines, *God and the Gay Christian*
Mel White, *Stranger at the Gate*

Of Particular Interest
to United Methodists

Phillip Cramer and William Harbison, *The Fight for Marriage*
Rueben Job and Neil Alexander, editors, *Finding Our Way: Love and Law
    in The United Methodist Church*
Kenneth Carter, *Embracing the Wideness*
**Karen Oliveto, *Our Strangely Warmed Hearts*

NOTES

Prologue

1. I am writing this book at a time when discussions are underway about better ways to refer to nonheterosexual persons. For purposes of simplicity and uniformity, I have used the LGBTQ designation, but I use this term to include people of all different sexual orientations.

2. Steve Harper, *For the Sake of the Bride: Restoring the Church to Her Intended Beauty* (Nashville: Abingdon, 2014). This book describes the experience I had in Lent of 2014 that caused me to change my heart and mind with respect to sexuality, and it offers three ways for Christians to find unity amid their differences about sexuality: love, nonjudgment, and holy conferencing.

1. The Journey

1. I am deliberately using verbs that describe continuing action. As with all aspects of my theological formation, God isn't finished with me yet. This book is an interim report from the field of lived experience. With respect to sexuality and every other aspect of my faith, I am (as E. Stanley Jones so often said) "a Christian under construction."

2. About a year after I wrote *For the Sake of the Bride* I was invited to speak at a conference sponsored by the Reconciling Ministries Network of The United Methodist Church. I was asked to speak on the topic "How I Changed My Mind." That address is available on YouTube under the title "Draw the Circle Wider," posted on March 2, 2015, https://www.youtube.com/watch?v=2ayOkX7oRm0.

3. I am intentionally not calling it an *orthodox* understanding, for orthodoxy is defined by the historic creeds of the Christian faith, and none of them mention sexuality. I am also intentionally not using the term *traditional* (even though some conservatives use it today), because my firsthand study of sexuality reveals that there has not been a singular view or voice in the church over two thousand years to the extent that conservatives would have us believe. We are living more under the influence of "traditionalism" (any view alleged to be more traditional than it actually is) than by the witness of the longstanding Christian tradition itself, which is more diverse (on almost every aspect of theology) than "traditionalists" allege.

4. In 1983, my friend Ira Gallaway put this growing sentiment into print in his book *Drifted Astray* (Nashville: Abingdon, 1983), writing a broad-spectrum critique of the mainline church with a no-holds-barred sentiment, going so far as to declare that liberal Christianity in general, and The United Methodist Church in particular, had abandoned the faith and substituted it with a human counterfeit he characterized as modernistic rationalism. In the circles I was running in, it was "a shot heard 'round the world." Conservatives preached sermons related to it, and churches studied it in order to know what was wrong with the church and what could be done about it.

5. This is important. It illustrates the institutional shift that Asbury Seminary has taken since then, becoming more closely aligned with the Good News movement, the Confessing Movement, the Institute for Religion and Democracy, and most recently the Wesleyan Covenant Association—where trustees, administrators, and faculty (and former presidents) hold offices and provide influence. Asbury Seminary has always been conservative, but over time it has become more fundamentalist in its mindset, in ways similar to the increasing fundamentalism within evangelical Christianity. When I was there as a student from 1970 to 1973 and for a season upon my return in 1980, it was not that way. Theology and ethos had become markedly different when I retired at the end of 2012.

6. Phyllis Tickle, *Emergence Christianity* (Grand Rapids: Baker Books, 2012). She wrote this book to summarize the movement as it was at that time. Needless to say, it has continued to evolve, with a family tree that now includes the Wild Goose Festival, the Poor People's Campaign, Fresh Expressions, the New Monasticism, and so forth.

7. One early indication that I was changing came through my book *Fresh Wind Blowing* (Eugene, OR: Cascade Books, 2013). It was not about sexuality but about living in God's new Pentecost, as many were doing, and still are.

8. That journey since 2014 has included upward of seven thousand pages of reading, both in affirming and nonaffirming literature. But more than that, it has included being befriended by LBGTQ people, when others were walking away. In the end, it has been relationships, not readings, that have been at the heart of this leg of the journey.

9. Harper, *For the Sake of the Bride,* xi–xiii.

69

10. Harper, *For the Sake of the Bride,* 1–4.

11. The hymn "And Can It Be?" written by Charles Wesley in 1739, about a year after he and John had their transforming experiences: Charles on May 21, 1738, on Marylebone Street, and John on May 24, 1838, on Aldersgate Street.

2. The Hermeneutic

1. Dr. Robert Traina was my primary professor in this learning. He did not invent the method, but he was a second-generation teacher of it, having studied with those who made the method prominent in theological education. He was a master teacher. His book *Methodical Bible Study* (privately published in 1952) was the standard text in the field, and it is still available under the title *Inductive Bible Study* (Grand Rapids: Baker Academic, 2011). Another seminal book was Oletta Wald's *The Joy of Discovery* (also privately published and undated); it too remains in print.

2. Through subsequent learning, I have come to see that IBS is on the family tree where we also find *lectio divina*. I visited with Dr. Traina about this, and he acknowledged the relationship. For fifty years, I have profited from the interplay between these two ways of reading and interpreting scripture.

3. Steve Harper, *For the Sake of the Bride: Restoring the Church to Her Intended Beauty* (Nashville: Abingdon, 2014), chapter 14.

4. Traina, *Methodical Bible Study*, 14.

5. This interpretation of the biblical revelation as a whole is something I share with others, including John Wesley, who spoke about "a religion of love" again and again. By getting my interpretive process straight, I have been able to integrate scripture, tradi-

70

tion, reason, and experience in ways I was unable to do when I began with the little passages before discovering the big picture. And with this new approach, I have been guided by others like Walter Brueggemann (who writes extensively about love as the core of covenant) and Elaine Heath, whose chapter "A Hermeneutic of Love" in her book *The Mystic Way of Evangelism* (Grand Rapids: Baker Academic, 2008) has helped me see what a theology of love looks like and how it is best shared with others.

6. Eugene Peterson, *The Message: The Bible in Contemporary Language* (Carol Stream, IL: NavPress, 2002), 19. This quotation comes from his introduction to the book of Genesis. Peterson's introductions have been as insightful for me as his rendering of the biblical text. They are gems.

7. I found Temple's statement in Dennis Kinlaw's book *Let's Start with Jesus* (Grand Rapids: Zondervan, 2005), 18.

8. Walter Brueggemann, *Theology of the Old Testament* (Minneapolis: Fortress, 2009), 215ff.

9. For more on these two words see William Mounce's *Complete Expository Dictionary of Old and New Testament Words* (Grand Rapids: Zondervan, 2006), 426–29.

10. Gregory of Nyssa, *The Life of Moses* (New York: Paulist, 1978), xv.

11. John Duns Scotus gave Francis's spirituality its theological substance. Karl Rahner provided an excellent summary of Scotism in *The Encyclopedia of Theology* (London: Burns and Oats, 1975), 1548.

12. Julian of Norwich, *Revelations of Divine Love* (available in multiple editions), chapter 86, epilogue.

13. Pierre Teilhard de Chardin, *Human Energy* (New York: Harcourt Brace Jovanovich, 1969), 72.

14. Louis Savary, *The New Spiritual Exercises: In the Spirit of Pierre Teilhard de Chardin* (Mahwah, NJ: Paulist, 2010), xi. He and his wife, Patricia Berne, have coauthored an excellent overview about this, *Teilhard de Chardin on Love* (Mahwah, NJ: Paulist, 2017).

15. Richard Rohr, *The Universal Christ* (New York: Convergent Books, 2019), 13. By "visible" he does not mean only that which we see with our eyes, but also the micro and macro expressions of creation the sciences are learning more and more about—a learning, he notes, that makes the whole thing even more mysterious and marvelous.

16. Unfortunately, the conservative interpretations of sexuality frequently fail to take into account the mountain of data coming to us from the natural and behavioral sciences. And some that do mention the discoveries do so using the term *junk science* as an attempt to explain away what nobody else does. We are in the mess we are in regarding sexuality partly (largely) because the conservative view has not incorporated insights from the sciences into its theology, leaving the theological message based in a scientific anthropology no longer held by the scientific community itself. For more about this, consult the references I offer in the "Reason" section of the bibliography at the end of the book.

17. This a pivotal point for interpreting sexuality. Austen Hartke wrote a helpful article about it in *The Christian Century*, "God's Unclassified World," April 25, 2018.

18. Kunal Das, *The Quantum Rules* (New York: Skyhorse, 2015). The book is a broad survey of quantum physics, but the author includes an application of physics to sexuality in chapter thirteen.

19. Ian Walmsley, *Light: A Very Short Introduction* (New York: Oxford University Press, 2015).

20. The allegation of a binary creation is a pivotal point for conservatives. N. T. Wright noted it in an interview published by *First Things* on June 11, 2014, https://www.firstthings.com/blogs/firstthoughts/2014/06/n-t-wrights-argument-against-same-sex-marriage. The binary view flows into a further interpretation of LGBTQ people as having, as a result of the fall, a distorted human nature. Wright spoke of this at a pastors' retreat in California in 2009, now available as a video posted online by Missio Alliance on September 9, 2013. However, a nonbinary understanding of creation removes any notion of LGBTQ distortion from the biblical revelation of human nature.

21. Richard Rohr, *The Divine Dance* (New Kensington, PA: Whitaker House, 2016), 51, 55.

22. One of the reasons is based on the linkage of sexuality with procreative capacity. This was obviously necessary for Adam and Eve; otherwise the human race would not have continued. But even before the end of Genesis 11, the necessity no longer existed because of the sheer volume of human beings. And today, the necessity does not exist, given roughly 90 percent of human beings are heterosexual. Moreover, the Church has never made procreative capacity a prerequisite for marriage. To turn around and use procreation as a case against LGBTQ sexuality is to topple a straw person.

23. Refer to the "Sciences" subsection in the "Reason" category of the bibliography for much more detail about the biological diversity now recognized in humanity—a diversity that we see when we look at gender, identify, and orientation.

24. This is the number I have found repeated in articles having to do with species on the earth today.

25. Mounce, *Complete Expository Dictionary*, 300–302. I have come to believe that the word *good* (*toba, tob*) is the thread of morality running through the rest of the Bible in its 597 uses in the Old Testament and the corresponding words *agathos* and *kalos* (with a combined use of 240 times) in the New Testament. These words are the basis for other important Bible words: *holiness, righteousness,* and so on. The idea of goodness is a major thread running through the Bible.

26. This will seem a harsh conclusion to draw from a view that an LGBTQ identity is a distortion of humanity, but it is one I have sadly confirmed through reading studies about this and through conversations with LGBTQ people whose friends took their lives when they became convinced they were somehow less than fully human. Their anxiety is amplified by some Christians who not only treat them as such (sometimes going so far as to call them abominations), but then go even further to tell them it is the way God feels about them as well. It is my opinion that this is one way we fail to heed Jesus's warning that we must not cause "little ones" (a word in Greek that means those who are marginalized and disrespected) to stumble (Mark 9:42).

27. Eknath Easwaran, *Original Goodness: A Commentary on the Beatitudes* (Tomales, CA: Niligri, 2017).

28. Thomas Merton, *New Seeds of Contemplation* (New York: New Directions, 1961), 60.

29. Israel's failure to fulfill this mission contributed largely to the need for a new covenant. Israel heard the word *chosen* to mean special, when God meant it to mean servant. The intended sense of universal belovedness deteriorated into a religious/political

imperialism rooted in the nation's distorted sense of itself. The prophets were sent to set the people free from this egocentric/ethnocentric bondage, but by and large the nation refused to change.

30. Brueggemann, *Theology of the Old Testament*, 216.

31. James Brownson, *Bible, Gender, and Sexuality* (Grand Rapids: Eerdmans, 2013), 139–40.

32. Mark Achtemeier, *The Bible's Yes to Same-Sex Marriage: An Evangelical's Change of Heart* (Louisville: Westminster John Knox, 2014). Achtemeier develops his thought across the pages of his book, not in a single section. He also has a good description of celibacy in scripture.

33. Philip F. Cramer and William Harbison, *The Fight for Marriage* (Nashville: Abingdon, 2018). These two lawyers were among those bringing cases to the United States Supreme Court that resulted in the 2015 landmark decision permitting same-gender marriage. The book is a fascinating account of how theology and law intertwine with respect to marriage. On pages 18–21, they show how a gender differentiation ceased to be a requirement.

34. These two dynamics (lifelong celibacy and prohibition of LGBTQ marriage) are additional illustrations of how we cause people to stumble (Mark 9:42). By requiring what scripture doesn't, we cut off an expression of sexuality for LGBTQ people that we grant to heterosexual people. Closing this pathway creates temptations for LGBTQ people to engage in sexual behavior that they themselves (particularly if they are Christian) do not view as legitimate. In other words, some in the Christian community are the ones who make the lives of LGBTQ people untenable in ways the Bible never requires.

35. Cheryl B. Anderson, *Ancient Laws and Contemporary Controversies* (New York: Oxford University Press, 2009). By using the Old Testament, the New Testament, church history, and Christian ethics, Anderson builds a convincing case for a hermeneutic of inclusion.

36. I have used E. Stanley Jones's terms *excarnate Christ* and *incarnate Christ* for a long time. Given the resurgence of interest and scholarship around the Christ, it has become a helpful way for me to write about Christian theology in general and sexuality in particular.

37. E. Stanley Jones, *In Christ* (Nashville: Abingdon, 1961), week 40, Saturday.

38. St. Athanasius, *The Incarnation of the Word of God* (New York: MacMillan, 1951), VII, "The Refutation of the Gentiles," 45. This work is also entitled *De Incarnatione Verbi* and *On the Incarnation*. It is available in both traditional and ebook editions.

39. Nowhere in the Bible is the connection between the creator and the cosmos better acknowledged, and that in a prescientific milieu. The perspective of biblical writers is a theological way of describing what contemporary cosmologists are discovering at both the micro and macro levels.

40. The Hebrew word translated "favor" means an action of acceptance and inclusion—of all. It is a word revealing that this is the disposition of God toward everyone—a disposition already seen in the creator, creation, and covenant sections of this chapter, and now, seen in Christ.

41. Of course, it includes physicality when it is used in relation to marriage. But the fact that it is used in nonmarital ways shows that its fundamental meaning is not sexual. See Gen 29:14; Judg 9:2; and 2 Sam 19:11-12.

42. Megan K. DeFranza, *Sex Difference in Christian Theology: Male, Female, and Intersex in the Image of God* (Grand Rapids: Eerdmans, 2015) looks at intersex people in detail and in relation to Christian theology.

43. The fact that Jesus does not mention homosexual people is called an argument from silence. In the scholarly world, it doesn't prove something one way or the other. But it is at least worth pointing out that here was an occasion ripe with opportunity to have spoken against homosexual people and same-sex marriages—and Jesus did neither.

44. Jones, *In Christ*, week 40, Saturday.

3. The Passages

1. Some conservatives have attempted to close the case on male/female sexuality and marriage by using the heavenly marriage image. But it fails to deliver on two fronts. First, the excarnate Christ (not the incarnate male Jesus) is the bridegroom—the eternal being who is without gender. And second, the bride (the church) is made up of many members, people of multiple genders, identities, and orientations. The Christ/Bride metaphor is beautiful, and it is a sign of a final union, but it is not literally or exclusively a male/female reality.

2. Kevan Wylie, "Sexuality: It's Not Just Sex," *Journal of the Royal Society of Medicine* (July 2007): 300–301.

3. William Mounce, *Complete Expository Dictionary of Old and New Testament Words* (Grand Rapids: Zondervan, 2006), 549. Another helpful study is found in *The New International Dictionary of New Testament Theology—Abridged Edition,* ed. Verlyn Verbrugge (Grand Rapids: Zondervan, 2003), 12.

77

4. I served on the Board of Ordained Ministry in the Florida Annual Conference of The United Methodist Church. Clergy sexual misconduct was almost entirely heterosexual sin. On one occasion I asked an Orange County deputy sheriff what percentage of sex crimes were committed by LGBTQ people. He did not have data to give me, but from his experience as a police officer for more than twenty years, he estimated no more than 2 percent. Another sobering fact is that LGBTQ people experience bullying, violence, and assault at a higher rate than heterosexual people—predominantly committed by heterosexual people.

5. N. T. Wright acknowledged this in the video I previously cited—comments he made at a pastor's retreat in California in 2009 and later posted on the Missio Alliance website in 2013.

6. Because I am a Christian in the Wesleyan tradition, in addition to the general comments that I will make about the five prohibitive passages, I will use footnotes to state John Wesley's view in relation to each of them, using his comments from *Explanatory Notes upon the Old Testament* (1765) and *Explanatory Notes upon the New Testament* (1755). These volumes are now often combined in one source, and they remain available in traditional and ebook formats.

7. Sidebar article in *The CEB Study Bible* (Nashville: Abingdon, 2013), 184OT.

8. The two verses are written against the backdrop of a complex social and religious milieu of Egyptian and Canaanite sexuality—a milieu beyond the scope of this book. For further study read Joshua Mark, "Love, Sex, and Marriage in Ancient Egypt," *Ancient History Encyclopedia*, September 26, 2016, https://www.ancient.eu/article/934/love-sex-and-marriage-in-ancient-egypt/, and "Canaanite Religion," *New World Encyclopedia*, March 8,

2019, http://www.newworldencyclopedia.org/entry/Canaanite _Religion.

9. Mounce, *Complete Expository Dictionary*, 403.

10. John Wesley does not comment on either of these verses.

11. Sexual orientation is complicated, but even more so when we try to interface our understandings of it today with ancient times. There was clearly same-sex behavior in ancient times, and people knew about it. But then, as now, there was no singular view about it or universal moral standard related to it. Judaism set the boundaries in relation to promiscuity, not orientation as the verses in Leviticus reveal.

12. The specific focus likely relates to promiscuous sexuality practiced in relation to fertility religion, and this may account for why women are not mentioned. Canaanite fertility religion was advanced through male sexual practices, not female—which is also an indicator of the inferior status of women in that day.

13. I am dealing with these two verses before turning to Romans because Paul likely wrote the letter to the Corinthians before he wrote to the Romans. First Timothy came along later, but because the issue there is essentially the same as with 1 Corinthians, I am treating them together.

14. John Wesley connected the idea of "softness" with indulgence and excess, not sexual behavior or orientation.

15. Craig Williams, *Roman Homosexuality* (New York: Oxford University Press, 2010), 145.

16. William Barclay, *The Daily Study Bible: The Letters to the Corinthians* (Philadelphia: Westminster, 1954), 58.

17. Robin Scroggs, *The New Testament and Homosexuality* (Philadelphia: Augsburg Fortress, 1984), 101–9.

18. The Sibylline Oracles, 2.70-77. But whether sexual or otherwise, *arsenokoitai* were people who abused others. The Oracles were written by Jewish and Christian writers from ca. 150 BCE to ca.180 CE.

19. Paul's travels are not easy to map. He apparently ministered in Corinth, left there to minister elsewhere, and wrote his letters back to them, and then returned to Corinth around the time that he wrote his letter to the Romans.

20. *The CEB Study Bible* has an excellent introduction to the letter.

21. This description may reinforce the idea among some scholars that ancient Canaanite deities had been carried over into Roman polytheism. If so, this makes the textual linkage between Leviticus and Romans even more interesting. Paul came out of Judaism with an already heightened resistance to idolatry wherever and however he found it.

22. Here is another interpretive mistake, i.e., focusing on the one sexual sin to the neglect of the others that Paul adds in verses 29-32. Paul has much more in mind than sinful sexuality in this passage. He shows how lustful idolatry leads to all sorts of things—some things Christians are much more prone to commit than sexual sin. But by making this passage a prohibition of LGBTQ sexual behavior, the larger impact and message gets lost.

23. James Brownson, *Bible, Gender, and Sexuality* (Grand Rapids: Eerdmans, 2013). He explores this in detail throughout the book; see the index references for "Unnatural." He rightly points out the difficulty of interpreting the word when trying to link its historic and contemporary meanings. But he does agree that the view Paul is speaking against heterosexual misconduct is plausible within the context of the passage being explored.

24. John Stott, *Homosexual Partnerships* (Downers Grove, IL: InterVarsity, 1985), 11. Stott calls the Roman behaviors "perversions," which means heterosexuals acting like homosexuals.

25. Brownson, *Bible, Gender, Sexuality*, 228–29.

4. The Life

1. "A Conversation with Walter Brueggemann," interview by Bradford Winters, *Image Journal*, issue 55 (undated), https://imagejournal.org/article/conversation-walter-brueggemann/.

2. Lawrence Mayer and Paul McHugh, "Sexuality and Gender," *Atlantis Journal* 50 (Fall 2016). Mayer and McHugh are professors of psychiatry at Johns Hopkins University. Their work is considered among the best regarding the formation of gender identity. Other helpful writings include "Gender Identity Is in the Brain. What Does This Tell Us?," by Joe Hebert in *Psychology Today*, August 10, 2016, https://www.psychologytoday.com/us/blog/hormones-and-the-brain/201608/gender-identity-is-in-the-brain-what-does-tell-us, and "Anatomy Does Not Determine Gender, Experts Say," by Denise Grady in *The New York Times*, October 22, 2018, https://www.nytimes.com/2018/10/22/health/transgender-trump-biology.html.

3. Here is another place where longitudinal studies are adding hard data to narrative. The Human Rights Campaign has links to a variety of studies, some done at universities and others done by The Centers for Disease Control and Prevention. It is impossible to read this information and listen to the stories of LGBTQ people and conclude that Christians have not harmed them.

4. The Pace e Bene ministry has been a nexus for guiding me to a knowledge of both effective nonviolent resistance actions and

to over fifty people (the list is growing) who have utilized them and are doing so today.

5. I have written more about this in my book *Living in Love* (Amazon, 2016).

6. Richard Rohr, *The Eight Core Principles* (Cincinnati: Franciscan Media, 2013), loc. 212. This is the third core principle of the Center for Action and Contemplation.

7. Martin Luther King Jr., *Strength to Love* (New York: Harper and Row, 1963). The whole book expands on the phrase and shows how theoretically and practically we minister with humility and compassion in the face of great challenges.

8. E. Stanley Jones, *Christian Maturity* (Nashville: Abingdon, 1978).

9. Ilia Delio, *The Unbearable Wholeness of Being: God, Evolution, and the Power of Love* (Maryknoll, NY: Orbis, 2013), 203.

10. Karen P. Oliveto, *Our Strangely Warmed Hearts* (Nashville: Abingdon, 2018), 128.

38764219R00050

Made in the USA
Lexington, KY
10 May 2019